SPRING PLEASURES

DATE DUE			
GAYLORD 234		PRINTED IN U.S.A.	

SPRING PLEASURES

A Southern Seasons Book

Martha Phelps Stamps

A CUMBERLAND HOUSE HEARTHSIDE BOOK

Nashville, Tennessee

Published by Cumberland House Publishing, Inc.
431 Harding Industrial Drive, Nashville, Tennessee 37211

Design by Gore Studio, Inc., Nashville, Tennessee.
Photography by Meryl Truett.

Library of Congress Cataloging-in-Publication Data

Stamps, Martha Phelps, 1961–
    Spring pleasures : menus and recipes that celebrate the beauty
and freshness of spring / Martha Phelps Stamps.
        p. cm.
    Includes index.
    ISBN 1-58182-009-7 (pbk. : alk. paper)
    1. Cookery, American—Southern style. I. Title.
    TX715.2.S68 S824   1999
    641.5975—dc21   99-17127
                                                          CIP

Printed in the United States of America
1 2 3 4 5 6 7 — 03 02 01 00 99

For John Mark,
and our new beginning.

Contents

7

CONTENTS

CONTENTS

CONTENTS

Introduction

Welcome to *The Southern Seasons*, a series of books that lives in and cooks with each particular season in a place called home. Local, seasonal food is important to me on a few levels. Eating in harmony with the rhythms of earth puts you that much closer to nature. God provides for us with beauty and bounty in each of the seasons. In recent decades, farming, groceries, and our very existence have become more regulated, more homogenous due to larger production and larger management. Most of us eat produce and farm stock that is shipped and trucked clear across the nation, either adding the enormous cost of air freight, or compromising the quality of product by picking too green or spraying with chemicals to sustain "freshness." The individual, the unique has been the victim. Whether it is the scuppernong grape, which everyone in these hills once gathered and is now nearly impossible to find; or the small farmer, who now gets paid to grow tobacco instead of wholesome, native food crops; or the dairies or small smoke houses, or graineries that closed down when the huge national ones shut them out. Buying locally supports your home's economy and ecology.

Eating and cooking with a local and seasonal sensibility is simply a treat. I love to scour the local farmers' market for gifts from the earth. My earth. The earth around here. Don't give me asparagus in October, or peaches at Christmas. Each season has its unique blessing, its own treats. And if you listen closely, your tummy (and your soul) are usually yearning for just what the earth is providing. Sweet potatoes, squash and pumpkin in the fall. Cabbage and turnips, hearty stews and starches come winter. In the spring I crave a tonic of fresh greens and wild things; and in the summer make it light, with lots of fresh fruit and simply cooked vegetables. *The Southern Seasons* celebrates the uniqueness of all of the times of the earth, with menus inspired by the bounty at hand.

SPRING PLEASURES

SPRING

Spring is intent on play. She's a breathy, giggly, frivolous girl. Now is the time to act on an impulse, whatever the consequence. In springtime the worst curmudgeons are given to illogical acts of kindness and sudden fits of laughter. Once stern teachers recite poetry on the lawn, and bankers sneak outside to bask in a bit of sun. For a brief spell each year, we are children again, all of us.

Children are Springtime's enchanted toys. She turns their noses yellow as they poke into daffodils and offers fields of violets to clutch in tiny fists. She crowns their heads with clover rings, the rulers of the day.

This is a time of innocence and wide-eyed discovery.

It seems that we all appreciate the precious nature of the spring. We throw fancy parties and dress in our Sunday Best. We give elegant tea parties for no reason at all. Even our food is at it's prettiest. Think of the vibrant greens of peas and asparagus and the pinks of rhubarb, raspberries, and strawberries.

I often use flowers as garnish and flavoring: chive blossoms, pansies, violets, and lavender. What I can't eat I bring into my home as each week's new offering: the brilliance of forsythia, then redbud and dogwood branches. Next come the heady aromas of lilac and lilies of the valley, followed by peonies and magnolia blossoms, feasts of sight and scent. Spring reveals each of her gifts, then suddenly, she's gone.

Don't waste a moment. Revel in all of her charms.

MARCH

*M*arch is fickle. She woos us with soft blue skies and tender green shoots, then shuts us in the deep freeze, just because she can. We try not to succumb to her wily ways. At the first day's warmth we knowingly say, "We mustn't get used to this." So she teases us with more. The daffodils sway and hyacinths burst forth with their curious form and heady scent. The school girls roll their sleeves up high, anxious for color on skin. We sigh. We relax. We start to get used to her gentle ways. . . . So she turns on us, or maybe turns her back, leaving us shivering and wiser, miserable in overcoats we loved so much just weeks before. It's a game, and Nature holds all the cards. Keeps us on our toes.

We search for foods to match our spring-like moods, but pickings are slim. The plants are wiser than we are. They take their time leaving the ground. The first crops are the bravest. Spinach, dandelion, and bitter greens, fennel, spring onions, beets, and rhubarb lend a strong character to early spring foods. They cleanse our senses like a tonic, preparing us for games ahead.

I.

A Time to Forage

When the brown and grey tangle of last year's leaves give way to tender sprouts of green, the heart gives way to it's own cravings. We are all innocent again, exuberant as Bambi. I, too want to forage in the underbrush for supplest sprouts and nibble at their promise.

Sallie's a forager, too. On one early spring visit from college she shared her discovery with me. I marveled at the sight and scent of the unfurled tendrils of our backyard ferns sautéing in sweet browned butter. Daddy refused to try them and never quite forgave Sallie for raiding his sacred plants. I tried them. Bright and slightly bitter, with a pleasant crunch. I forage, too, but when the spring calls me to forage, I go a bit deeper in the woods than Sallie did that day. The youngest always learns from the eldest's transgressions.

Daddy has his own spring craving. Poke salet. This proliferous weed is now not commonly eaten in the South, but Daddy adores it. We had it as often as we had turnip greens growing up. That's often enough. I'm his only child that developed a taste for poke. The leaves become slightly toxic, and brilliant, poisonous purple berries grow as poke salet matures. Tender young plants are the ones you want.

The Menu

Savory Spring Tart

———

Smoked Trout with Beet and Grapefruit

———

Almond Nests with Lime Curd and Fresh Raspberries

Savory Spring Tart

Of course an individual not given to foraging could substitute dandelion, spinach, curly endive or young kale or mustard greens. A more daring individual might choose to substitute wild ramps for the onions.

Fiddleheads can be found at many specialty grocers. Using wild mushrooms instead would make an altogether different, but equally delicious pie.

SERVES 6 TO 8

FOR THE CRUST:
¾   cup all-purpose flour
1   teaspoon salt
½   cup cornmeal
½   cup (1 stick) cold unsalted butter, cut in small
        pieces
2   tablespoons shortening
        About 3 tablespoons ice water

FOR THE FILLING:
⅔   pound baby spinach leaves, dandelion greens, or
        poke salet
2   or 3 small spring onions
¼   cup (½ stick) butter
⅓   pound fiddlehead ferns (or wild mushrooms,
        sliced)
½   teaspoon salt
½   teaspoon white pepper
        Juice of 1 lemon
4   eggs

Pinch grated nutmeg
Salt and white pepper to taste
½ *pound feta cheese, crumbled*
1 *cup milk or cream*

In a large bowl stir together the flour, salt, and cornmeal. Use your fingers or a pastry knife to deftly work the butter and shortening into the dry ingredients, working quickly and lightly until the dough resembles a coarse meal. Dribble the ice water over the dough and work with your hands or a rubber spatula until you have a shaggy dough that holds together. Gather the dough and press into a disk. Wrap in plastic wrap and refrigerate. Refrigerate while you prepare the filling, or for at least 1 hour and up to 2 days. May also be frozen and thawed in the refrigerator.

Clean the greens well. Slice the onions in thin circles. In a sauté pan heat the butter. Add the onions and fiddleheads or mushrooms and cook for about 1 minute to soften. Add the spinach, salt, and pepper, and cook to wilt the spinach. Squeeze in the lemon and cook until most of the liquid has evaporated, just a few minutes more. Set aside. In a bowl mix together the eggs with additional salt, pepper, and the nutmeg.

Preheat the oven to 375°. Roll out the pastry dough and line a greased pie or tart pan. Loosely place the spinach and onion mixture in the pastry. Crumble the cheese over this and pour the cream and egg mixture over all. Poke around a bit to evenly distribute the egg mixture. Bake for about 45 minutes until the center is puffed and set.

Smoked Trout with Beet and Grapefruit

This is a beautiful salad, with lots of intriguing flavors. I use pecan smoked trout, made locally by my friend Butch from Bucksnort. Butch's trout is the best I've ever tasted, rich and complex, but any good smoked trout will do.

SERVES 6 TO 8

3	grapefruit
1	medium-sized beet
2	tablespoons champagne or white wine vinegar
2	tablespoons best-quality olive oil
4	smoked trout fillets
1	tablespoon minced fresh tarragon, or other fresh, tender herb, such as dill or parsley

Using a sharp chef's knife, cut the peel and pith from the grapefruit, leaving it whole. Working over a bowl, use a sharp paring knife to remove the sections, cutting down one side of a section and pushing out the other. Peel the beet, then continue using the peeler to make ribbons (you may want to wear rubber gloves—beets will stain your hands for a while). Add the beet ribbons to the grapefruit. Add the vinegar and toss.

Remove the skin from the trout. Break the trout in large pieces and divide amongst individual salad plates. Spoon some of the grapefruit and beets to the side of the trout. Garnish with the tarragon and serve.

Almond Nests with Lime Curd and Fresh Raspberries

A nice, light dessert to end the meal. Too much dessert at lunch and I have to nap, then I wake up grumpy.

MAKES ABOUT 8 TO 10 SERVINGS

ALMOND MERINGUE NESTS:
1   cup blanched almonds
6   egg whites, at room temperature
½   teaspoon salt
1½   teaspoons cream of tartar
1½   cups sugar
     Lime Curd (recipe follows)
1   pint fresh raspberries

Preheat the oven to 250°. Line a baking sheet with ungreased brown paper, such as from a grocery bag.

In a food processor finely grind the almonds.

Place the egg whites in a clean bowl. Add the salt and cream of tartar and beat to a soft peak. Alternately add the almonds and sugar in small batches, beating well after each addition until the whites are glossy. Use a large spoon to scoop out the meringue and place onto the prepared baking sheet in a 3- to 4-inch circle, making a depression in the center. Bake for about 1 hour until the shells are hardened and ivory colored. Turn the oven off and leave the shells in the oven until completely cooled, at least 2 hours and up to overnight. Store covered until ready to use. They will last for several days.

To assemble the nests: Have on hand the meringues, the lime curd, and 1 pint of fresh raspberries. Place one meringue on each dessert plate. Spoon about 2 tablespoons of Lime Curd into each, then place a few raspberries on top. Serve at once.

Lime Curd

MAKES 1⅔ CUPS

8	egg yolks
⅓	cup sugar
	Grated zest of 1 lime
	Juice of 2 limes (about ½ cup)
6	tablespoons (¾ stick) unsalted butter, cut in small pieces

Place the egg yolks, sugar, and zest in a nonreactive saucepan. Whisk until light in color. Add the lime juice and butter and cook over medium heat, whisking until the butter is melted. Continue to cook, whisking constantly, until the mixture is thickened. Remove from the heat and strain through a mesh strainer into a bowl. The mixture will thicken more as it cools. Let cool, then cover and refrigerate. Keeps about 1 week.

2.

Mary's Birthday

My sister Mary's birthday comes at the perfect time of year for a party. We call it early spring, but it's really the hanging's on of winter. We've had several bright, daffodil days by then, but you can also wake up to gray and thick frost on your windshield. Fancy parties do much to lighten the spirits.

Now Mary likes a party. I appreciate that in her. Some people moan and complain and say, "Oh, don't go to any trouble." That's no fun. Once in a while we ought to go to some trouble. Like for someone's fortieth birthday, for example. Someone that taught you how to read and write when you were three. Someone who appreciates a good, fancy party.

This year on Mary's birthday, my sister Sallie's house was filled with lots of friends and laughter, and some great food.

The Menu

Steamed Asparagus

———

Buttermilk Blue Cheese Dip

———

Chicken Salad with Grapes and Walnuts in Pastry Cups

———

Orange Coconut Muffins with Country Ham

———

Smoked Trout Spread

———

Mama's Baby Cheesecakes

Steamed Asparagus

Mary loves asparagus even more than your average Nashvillian, and Nashville is an asparagus town. New Orleans is an artichoke town; we go for asparagus. When I was a child, the fancy cocktail form was a spear of canned asparagus wrapped in thinly rolled white bread that was spread with mayonnaise. This was slathered with melted butter (or oleo) and run under the broiler. Not too healthy, but a distinctive taste from my past. Fresh asparagus looks great just in time for Mary's birthday. Of course, these days, fresh asparagus looks great all the time. We are spoiled.

SERVES ABOUT 12 FOR A COCKTAIL BUFFET

2	pounds fresh asparagus
2	teaspoons fresh salt

Snap the asparagus stalks about a third up, where they break easily. Bring a gallon of water to boil with the salt (the salt keeps the asparagus, or any green vegetable, green). Have ready a large bowl of ice water. Place the trimmed asparagus in the boiling water and cook, uncovered, about 1 minute, until tender but firm to the bite. Drain the asparagus and place it in the ice water to stop the cooking. Keep in the ice water about 5 minutes, until quite cool. Drain and refrigerate until ready to serve.

Buttermilk Blue Cheese Dip

Thin a little and use as a salad dressing, or serve with grilled chicken or tenderloin.

MAKES 1 PINT

½   cup Hellman's mayonnaise (or homemade)
½   cup buttermilk
¾   cup crumbled blue cheese
      Juice of 1 lemon
2   cloves garlic, minced
¼   teaspoon cayenne
      Freshly cracked black pepper to taste

In a medium bowl mix everything together. Let sit for 30 minutes before serving to allow the flavors to marry. Taste for seasoning and serve. Store covered and refrigerated for up to a week.

Chicken Salad with Grapes and Walnuts in Pastry Cups

Phyllo pastry is widely available and extremely versatile. Don't be scared, it's really not hard to work with.

MAKES 12 SERVINGS

FOR THE PASTRY CUPS:

Olive oil

1   *package phyllo*

FOR THE SALAD:

6   *bone-in, skin-on chicken breasts*

1   *onion, quartered*

1   *carrot, quartered*

1   *bay leaf*

1   *teaspoon dried thyme*

Salt and pepper to taste

About 36 seedless red grapes, cut in half

2   *sticks celery, diced*

1   *cup toasted walnuts, broken in pieces*

⅓   *cup mayonnaise*

⅓   *cup sour cream*

4   *green onions, thinly sliced*

2   *teaspoons fresh tarragon*

Salt and pepper

Preheat the oven to 400°. Spray a muffin tin with nonstick spray. Clean a large work area.

To prepare the pastry cups, pour about ½ cup of olive oil in a cup. Unroll the phyllo. Cover it with a clean cloth if you have to pause. Lift off one sheet of phyllo and place it on the clean work surface. Use a pastry brush (I use a small paint brush) to lightly brush it with oil. Place another sheet on top and brush with oil. Repeat for two more layers. Use a paring knife to cut out twelve 4-inch circles from the phyllo sheets and fit these into the muffin tin. Bake for 10 minutes and let cool in the tin. Remove and store in an air tight container until ready to use. Don't fill until just before serving.

To prepare the salad, rinse the chicken breasts and place in a pot. Add the onion, carrot, bay leaf, thyme, salt, and pepper, and cover with water. Bring to a boil, turn heat down to simmer and cook about 20 minutes until the chicken is cooked through. Remove from the broth (be sure to save the broth for soup!) and let cool. Pull the meat from the bones in bite-sized chunks. Refrigerate while you prepare the rest of the salad.

In a large bowl mix together the grapes, celery, walnuts, mayonnaise, sour cream, green onions, tarragon, salt, and pepper. Stir in the chicken and taste for seasoning. Fill the phyllo cups with the salad just before serving. Makes enough for at least 12 muffin-sized pastry cups.

Orange Coconut Muffins with Country Ham

Sallie made these. The slightly sweet taste is delicious with the salty ham.

MAKES 12 REGULAR OR 36 MINI MUFFINS

1½   cups all-purpose flour
1   teaspoon baking powder
1   teaspoon baking soda
1   teaspoon ground cinnamon
1   teaspoon ground ginger
½   teaspoon salt
2   eggs
¾   cup sugar
1   cup shredded coconut
1   cup well-drained crushed pineapple
¼   cup orange juice
5   tablespoons vegetable oil

Butter for spreading
Country ham (about ¼ pound, thinly sliced)

Preheat the oven to 400°. Grease 12 regular or 36 mini muffin cups.

In a medium bowl whisk together the flour, baking powder, baking soda, cinnamon, ginger, and salt. In a separate bowl whisk together the eggs and sugar. Stir in the coconut, pineapple, and orange juice. Stir in the oil. Fold in the flour mixture just until moistened without over mixing. Divide evenly among the muffin cups. Bake about 15 minutes until browned, puffed, and cooked through. Let cool in the pan.

When cool enough to handle, split and stuff with soft butter and country ham.

Smoked Trout Spread

Sadly, Nashville is eight hours from the nearest ocean shore, but we are blessed with abundant freshwater lakes and rivers. The trout is plentiful and divine. My friend Butch in Bucksnort, Tennessee, has been smoking trout for local restaurants and specialty stores for over ten years. He just recently started smoking with pecan wood. I approve.

Check out locally smoked trout in your own area. I know there's great stuff in Idaho and Colorado, as well as the mountains of North Carolina. I believe in supporting the guy down the road. You could easily substitute smoked catfish, or a mild smoked salmon.

I first made this for a recent Christmas cocktail party. It was so simple, I kept thinking that I should be trying harder.

MAKES 1 QUART

2	smoked trout fillets
1	cup cream cheese
1	cup sour cream
1	cup heavy cream
½	small red onion, grated
	Juice of 1 lemon
2	teaspoons capers, chopped
1	tablespoon chopped parsley
	Cracked black pepper, to taste

Take the trout from the skin and process in a food processor. Add the remaining ingredients and process until smooth. Taste and adjust the seasoning. Refrigerate until ready to serve. Serve with crackers or toast points.

Mama's Baby Cheesecakes

This is a wonderful, quick dessert for a crowd. Petite and beautiful.

MAKES ABOUT 75 TINY PASTRIES

3	8-ounce packages cream cheese
5	eggs
1	cup plus ½ cup sugar
1½	teaspoons plus ¼ teaspoon almond extract
1	cup sour cream
1	jar seedless raspberry preserves

Preheat the oven to 300°. Line mini muffin tins with small paper liners. In a large bowl beat the cream cheese with an electric mixer. Add the eggs, 1 cup of sugar, and 1 ½ teaspoons of almond extract, and mix well. Fill the cups ¼ full with this mixture and bake for 20 minutes. Don't brown.

Meanwhile, mix together the sour cream with the remaining sugar and almond extract. Drop 1 teaspoon on each, then drop a bit of the raspberry jelly. Bake for another 5 to 10 minutes. Let cool in the pans. Refrigerate until ready to serve.

3

The Big Bug Boil

Crayfish season comes just at the end of Mardi Gras, depending on when it falls. I know this from working with my friend Steve Scalise who was born and raised in the heart of New Orleans. Steve is the very finicky keeper of the seafood case at The Corner Market. Each year we have a huge celebration with jambalaya, po boys, gumbo, and etouffée. There's always one or two customers who peer behind the counter and shout at Steve, "Are the crawfish in yet?" Steve taps his knife on the counter and shifts his weight. "Not chet, but they're comin'. I can feel 'em."

Evidently Steve has a spiritual umbilical cord connected to the swamp. He can feel the bugs, as they call them down there. He can feel the bugs as they begin to stir in still cool mud where they choose to winter.

In New Orleans, when the bugs come in folks roll up their sleeves. Up this way, we're usually still in jackets for the first of the bugs. This is a most opportune happenstance if you are the sort that likes a cookout. Julie and Joe and their three beautiful girls (also of Corner Market fame) host the big bug boils on their farm in the country. Hopefully the day is brisk, so you can stand near the fire eating hot bugs so spicy that you suck down a cold beverage to cool your own fire within. Extremities in temperature seem to quicken the blood.

The Menu

Crayfish Boil

———

Banana Bread Pudding

Crayfish Boil

My friend Meryl, who lives in Savannah, where "boils" are a cultural event, has a giant propane heated pot on a tripod. You can also heat a pot over an outdoor grill, or inside on top of the stove. If you don't have facilities or utensils for these numbers, use a large pasta pot with a slotted insert, and boil them in batches. Boil all of the vegetables at the beginning with the first batch. That way they'll flavor the cooking water and not get overdone. Of course you could cut the quantities, as well.

To feed a crowd

1	sack (about 40 pounds) crawfish
10	bags crab boil
3	ounces (2 jars) cayenne pepper
4	pounds salt
10	heads of garlic, cut in half cross-wise
12	lemons, cut in half
8	onions, cut in half
5	pounds new potatoes, rinsed
1	bunch celery, cleaned and separated
3	to 4 loaves French bread

Dump the live crawfish into a deep sink or very large pot. Fill with water. This will purge the crayfish. Discard dead ones. Meanwhile, get an enormous pot with 12 gallons of water to a boil with all the remaining ingredients except the bread. Boil the water with the seasoning for 10 minutes. Add the crawfish and boil for 10 minutes. Turn off the heat and let sit in the water for another 20 minutes. Drain and serve (they're great cold, too) with the bread to sop up the juices. Be sure to eat up the potatoes, celery, and onions, and to squeeze out the garlic cloves and spread them onto the bread as well. Heaven in springtime.

Banana Bread Pudding

A rich and soothing dessert to take the edge off of the heat.

SERVES 16 TO 20

2	loaves banana bread, cubed
4	eggs
1	cup firmly packed brown sugar
4	cups milk

Preheat the oven to 350°. Grease a large Pyrex or ceramic baking dish. Toss in the bread cubes. In a bowl whisk together the eggs and sugar. Whisk in the milk. Pour over the bread crumbs (at this point you may refrigerate the pudding for several hours, if you wish. Wait to preheat the oven until you're ready to bake). Bake uncovered for about 40 minutes until the pudding is set and lightly browned.

Options: Sprinkle the top with coconut or stir raisins or currants into the pudding.

4.

Soup for Supper

The early spring is flirtatious and sassy. She taunts us with the pinks of japonica branches and the emerald green of crocus leaves against purple and gold in the still gray grass, but the winds are bitter yet. We crave the new and fresh, while our bodies still need some warming. Now's the time for a good strong soup, but a clear one, light and vibrant—no cream soups now. Fish will do the trick, and perhaps some rice, all enveloped in an aromatic broth—a tonic, if you will, to dispel the last of the winter blues, and beckon in the spring. Invite some friends and enjoy the last fire in the fireplace while you dream of the months to come with the sunny flavors of an ocean tide.

The Menu

Carrot and Arugula Salad

———

Red Snapper Soup with Watercress and Fennel Tops

———

Mama's Pull Aparts

———

Dried Cherry Tart

Carrot and Arugula Salad

A fresh, light salad—very pretty, too.

SERVES 6

3	*fresh carrots*
1	*bunch arugula*
1	*tablespoon champagne or white wine vinegar*
1	*tablespoon olive oil*
	Salt and pepper to taste

Peel the carrots, then, working over a salad bowl, use the peeler to prepare the carrot in very thin ribbons. Toss with remaining ingredients and serve as a small first or side course.

Red Snapper Soup with Watercress and Fennel Tops

I grew fennel for the first time this year. While the bulbs are more aromatic, the feathery tops are fragrant, as well, and charming in a soup.

Snapper is one of my favorite fish, but any light-fleshed one will do.

SERVES 6 AS A MAIN COURSE

1	red onion
1	bulb fennel, with tops
3	cloves garlic
2	tablespoons olive oil
6	cups chicken stock
1	cup dry white wine
1	bay leaf
	Salt to taste
	Black, white, and red pepper to taste
1½	pounds red snapper fillet, or other white-fleshed fish
	Zest and juice of 3 lemons
¼	cup chopped watercress (or parsley)
1	medium tomato, diced
2	cups cooked white rice

Cut off the top and bottom the onion and slice in half through the top and bottom. Remove the skin and lay the onion cut side down on a cutting board. Slice thin strips lengthwise through each half. Core the fennel bulb and slice thinly. Set the fennel tops aside.

In a large stock pot heat the olive oil. Sweat the onion and sliced fennel bulb in the oil for about 5 minutes. Add the garlic and cook 1 more minute. Pour in the stock and wine, add the bay leaf, salt, and pepper and heat to a boil. Let boil about 5 minutes. Add the snapper and let the stock come back to a simmer. Reduce the heat and simmer about 5 minutes until the fish is just cooked.

Meanwhile, use a zester to remove the lemon zest in thin strips. Set aside. Cut the lemons in half and squeeze the juice through a strainer. Chop the fennel tops coarsely. Add the fennel and lemon juice to the soup along with the watercress and diced tomato. Simmer gently for 1 minute. Remove the bay leaf. Divide the rice among 6 soup bowls. Ladle the soup over the rice and top with the lemon zest.

Mama's Pull Aparts

This is made with choux pastry, the same type as cream puffs and eclairs. My mother started making these when I was in high school, something she had clipped from the newspaper. One bite and you're hooked.

SERVES 6 AS A SNACK

½	cup water
¼	cup (½ stick) butter, cut into bits
¼	teaspoon salt
½	cup all-purpose flour
3	eggs
¼	cup grated Gruyere or other fine Swiss-style cheese
	Fresh ground black pepper to taste
2	tablespoons heavy cream

Preheat the oven to 400°. Lightly spray a baking sheet with non-stick spray. In a small heavy saucepan place the water, butter, and salt, and bring to a boil. Add the flour all at once, stirring to a smooth dough. Remove from the heat and beat in the eggs one at a time, mixing well. Stir in the cheese and black pepper to taste.

For small and dainty pastries, spoon teaspoon-sized drops of the dough on the greased pan to form a circle roughly the diameter of a serving plate, then fill in the circle with teaspoon-sized drops of batter. Lightly brush the tops with the cream. Bake for about 30 to 40 minutes until risen, crisp, and lightly browned on top. Use a spatula to slide the ring of pastries onto a serving plate and serve at once.

Dried Cherry Tart

Cherries seem to breathe of spring, but that's the blossoms, not the fruit. Satisfy your cherry cravings with dried ones. Their burst of flavor is refreshing.

SERVES 6 TO 8

1	sheet puff pastry
½	cup sour cream
⅓	cup plus 4 teaspoons sugar
1	egg
	Grated zest of 1 orange
1	teaspoon almond extract
1	egg yolk
1	tablespoon milk
6	ounces dried cherries
½	cup Kirsh or other liqueur

Place a sheet of parchment paper on a clean work surface and lightly sprinkle with flour. Roll out the pastry to a ⅛-inch rectangle. Roll about 2 inches along the outside up and in, forming a lip. Move the parchment with pastry to a baking sheet. Refrigerate at least 30 minutes.

In a small bowl mix together the sour cream, ⅓ cup of sugar, egg, orange zest, and almond extract. Set aside. In a separate small bowl place the cherries and pour the Kirsh over. Set aside. Remove the crust from the refrigerator and prick all over with a fork. Mix together the egg yolk and milk, and paint the entire surface of the pastry with the mixture. With a rubber spatula spread the sour cream evenly in the bottom of the crust. Refrigerate the crust again for 20 minutes.

Preheat the oven to 425°. Remove the tart from the refrigerator. Drain the cherries and scatter them evenly over the sour cream mixture. Bake for 15 minutes, then sprinkle with the remaining sugar. Bake another 5 or 10 minutes until the center is set and the crust nicely browned. Serve warm or at room temperature.

Savory Spring Tart (page 21)

49

Steamed Asparagus with Buttermilk Blue Cheese Dip (page 29)

Banana Bread Pudding (page 40)

Red Snapper Soup with Watercress and Fennel Tops (page 44)

Veal and Artichoke Stew with Carrots and Dill (page 59)

Grilled Tuna over Baby Spinach with New Potatoes, Steamed Beans, Cheese Croutons, and Dijon Vinaigrette (page 67)

Baptism Cakes (page 83)

Sweet Potato and Beet Chips (page 88)

5.

Sunday Night Stew

Sunday night is my stew night. Stews are far from difficult, but they are a bit demanding of your time. The initial requirement is chopping, and then a stew just needs to take its own time. Time that I spend reading the paper, doing the laundry, mulching the flower beds—Sunday afternoon things. With the first promise of spring, my tastes do change. I still yearn for the comfort, the feel, the welcome of a stew, but a stew not quite robust, not quite, as we say 'round these parts, rib sticking. In fact, I require something that will not stick to my ribs at all, something more silken than velvet, something more tender than hearty. Veal is the ticket. Artichokes are the vehicle, and delicate fresh dill, the finishing touch. This stew speaks to the naïve rumblings we all hear as the land awakes again.

The Menu

Veal and Artichoke Stew with Carrots and Dill

———

Pea and Sugar Snap Salad

———

Spring Carrot Cake

———

Buttermilk Cream Cheese Frosting

Veal and Artichoke Stew with Carrots and Dill

You can use a less expensive cut of veal. Don't cook too long, or the meat will dry out.

SERVES 6

3	tablespoons plus 2 tablespoons olive oil
2	pounds veal cubes (from shoulder)
	Salt and white pepper to taste
1½	tablespoons plus 1½ tablespoons all-purpose flour
½	cup white wine
1	onion, diced large
1	carrot, peeled and diced large
3	cloves garlic, minced
3	to 4 cups chicken stock, heated
2	9-ounce boxes frozen artichoke hearts, thawed
1	tablespoon lemon juice
1	tablespoon minced fresh dill
1	package wide egg noodles

In a large heavy pot heat 3 tablespoons of the oil. Season the veal with salt and pepper, then dust with 1½ tablespoons of flour. Brown the veal all over in the hot oil, being careful not to over crowd the pot. Do this in batches, if necessary. Use a slotted spoon to remove the veal.

Deglaze the pan with the wine, scraping up the browned bits. Pour this over the reserved veal. Wipe out the pan and add 2 tablespoons of oil. Add the onion to the oil and cook about 5 minutes to wilt the onions. Add the carrot and garlic and cook for 2 or 3 minutes. Sprinkle the remaining flour over the vegetables and stir to coat well. Cook 1 or 2 minutes, then slowly pour in the hot stock, stirring. Bring to a boil, then turn down to simmer. Add the veal and cook about 20 minutes until tender.

Stir in the artichoke hearts and lemon and cook for 5 more minutes, until the artichoke hearts are heated through. Stir in the dill. Taste and adjust the seasoning.

Meanwhile, cook the egg noodles in plenty of boiling salted water until just tender. Drain and toss with a bit of olive oil. Serve the stew over the cooked egg noodles.

Pea and Sugar Snap Salad

Crisp and tender as the season.

SERVES 6

2	cups fresh or frozen peas, picked over
1	pound sugar snaps
2	scallions, thinly sliced (or 1 small spring onion, cut in thin circles
2	tablespoons olive oil
2	tablespoons champagne vinegar
	Salt and pepper to taste
1	tablespoon toasted sesame seeds

Bring a pot of salted water to a boil. Place the peas in a metal colander or steamer and submerge in the boiling water. Cook until just tender. Remove and shock in ice water.

Add the sugar snaps to the water and cook about 1 minute. Strain and shock in ice water.

In a large bowl mix together the olive oil, scallions, champagne vinegar, salt, and pepper. Drain the vegetables well and toss in the bowl. Serve garnished with sesame seeds.

Spring Carrot Cake

Somehow, the usual "spiciness" and heartiness of carrot cake has made me always associate it with the brisker months, but carrots, after all, are a spring crop. Draining the carrots makes for a much more flavorful cake, while limiting the spice to ginger lends a more exuberant feel.

SERVES 10 TO 12

2⅔   cups all-purpose flour
4   teaspoons baking powder
½   teaspoon baking soda
2   teaspoons ground ginger
1   teaspoon salt
2   pounds carrots, grated
1   cup plus ⅔ cups sugar
5   eggs
1   cup firmly packed light brown sugar
1   cup (2 sticks) butter, melted
¾   cup sweetened, shredded coconut
1½   teaspoons vanilla extract

Preheat the oven to 350°. Grease and flour two 9-inch round cake pans.

In a large bowl mix the flour with the baking powder, soda, ginger, and salt. Set aside.

Set a colander in a sink, or over a large bowl. In it, toss the grated carrot with 1 cup of the sugar. Let sit for 30 minutes, then press down on the carrots to release additional liquid.

Meanwhile, in a large bowl beat the eggs with the remaining sugar and brown sugar. Whisk in the melted butter, then stir in the flour mixture, and finally the carrots and coconut.

Divide the batter evenly between the pans. Bake in the center of the oven for about 45 minutes, until a cake tester inserted in the center comes out clean. Let cool in the pans for 10 minutes. Invert onto racks and let cool completely before icing.

Buttermilk Cream Cheese Frosting

FROSTS ONE 2-LAYER CAKE

2	8-ounce packages cream cheese, at room temperature
½	cup (1 stick) butter, at room temperature
2½	cups confectioners' sugar
1	tablespoon buttermilk
½	cup toasted coconut (optional)
½	cup toasted walnuts (optional)

In a medium bowl beat together the cream cheese and butter. Add the sugar and buttermilk and beat until smooth. Assemble and ice the cakes. Garnish with toasted coconut or toasted walnuts, if desired.

6.

Spring Break at the Gulf

Nashville vacations on a strip of beach known as the Florida panhandle. My parents became engaged in Destin in 1953, and my family spent a week at Ft. Walton every year for the better part of my youth. At times, eighty percent of the hotels in this area are occupied by Nashvillians. Spring break is one of these times. This is north Florida, so you run the risk of cool weather. Even so, the beaches are long expanses of powder white sand with high dunes lined in sea grass. The old bungalows have, for the most part, been replaced by high rises, but thoughtful planning has gone into communities such as Seaside, recently featured in the movie *The Truman Show*. Deck top grills provide the perfect excuse for a cookout of local seafood, prepared lightly and enjoyed out of doors.

The Menu

Grilled Tuna over Baby Spinach with New Potatoes,
Steamed Beans, Cheese Croutons, and Dijon Vinaigrette

———————

Frozen Banana Yogurt

Grilled Tuna over Baby Spinach with New Potatoes, Steamed Beans, Cheese Croutons, and Dijon Vinaigrette

Gulf tuna is a delicacy that is sadly growing more scarce. It grills beautifully, for even the novice. Marinating in olive oil keeps the fish nice and moist in the center.

SERVES 6

FOR THE TUNA:

6	6-ounce tuna fillets
½	cup olive oil
3	cloves garlic, minced
	Salt and black pepper
	Juice from lemons

FOR THE POTATOES:

1	pound red skin new potatoes
	Salt

FOR THE GREEN BEANS:

1	pound green beans
	Salt

FOR THE DIJON VINAIGRETTE:

2	cloves garlic
2	tablespoons dijon mustard
2	tablespoons red wine vinegar
1	teaspoon capers, drained and roughly chopped
4	tablespoons olive oil
2	tablespoons chopped fresh parsley

Salt and black pepper to taste

Cheese Croutons (recipe follows)
2   *pounds baby spinach*

Rinse the fillets and pat dry. In a large flat Pyrex or bowl mix together the olive oil, garlic, salt, and pepper. Place the fillets in the bowl, turning to coat well. Cover and let marinate, refrigerated, for at least 1 hour or up to 6 hours.

Prepare the grill to medium heat. Remove the fillets from the marinade and cook on the grill to medium doneness, about 4 minutes per side. Remove from the grill, place on a platter, and squeeze the lemon juice over. Let rest briefly while you assemble the salad

Clean the potatoes well. Place in a pot and cover with water. Add about a tablespoon of salt. Bring to a boil on top of the stove. Turn to medium and cook about 15 to 20 minutes until fork-tender. Drain and let cool in the colander without rinsing. Refrigerate until just before serving.

Place water in the bottom of a steamer or pot. Add two teaspoons of salt and bring to a simmer. Meanwhile, clean and string the beans. Place in the top portion of the steamer or in a colander that will fit snugly over the pot. Place over the simmering water, cover, and steam for about 6 minutes until tender. Remove and cool under cold running water. Set aside or refrigerate until just ready to serve.

Run the garlic through a press or mince quite finely. Place in a jar with a tight fitting lid. Add the remaining ingredients. Screw on the lid and shake well. Set aside or refrigerate until a little while before serving. Let come to room temperature before serving. Keeps in the refrigerator, covered, for about a week.

Toss the baby spinach and croutons with all but 2 tablespoons of the vinaigrette. (The spinach usually comes cleaned, and you just open the bag and toss. If not available, use mature spinach, taking care to clean and dry well.) Divide evenly among six dinner plates. Plate the just-grilled tuna over the spinach, and arrange the beans and potatoes on either side. Drizzle each with reserved vinaigrette and serve.

Cheese Croutons

Any hard, grating cheese that will grate easily would work here. I'm always looking for local and regional products, so I suggest a fabulous hard cheese made in Louisiana on Chicory Farms. Californian Dry Jack would also be great, or a Parmigiano Reggiano.

½   loaf French or sourdough bread
¼   cup olive oil
½   cup grated cheese
      Salt and pepper to taste

Preheat the oven to 375°. Cut the bread into cubes and place in a bowl. Add the olive oil and cheese and toss to coat. Turn onto a baking sheet and bake until nicely browned, about 10 minutes, turning to brown evenly. If you want to keep these around for a few days, bake them until they are completely dried out. You may need to lower the oven temperature. If you are eating them that night, though, I suggest serving them crunchy on the outside and still a little moist within.

Frozen Banana Yogurt

This is quick, easy, low-fat, and luscious. The perfect resort dessert.

MAKES 1 QUART

3	ripe bananas
	Juice of 1 lemon
½	cup honey
1	pint low-fat vanilla yogurt
½	teaspoon orange blossom water (optional)

Peel and place the bananas in a bowl with the lemon juice. Use a potato masher to mash. Stir in remaining ingredients. Pour into an ice cream maker and freeze according to the manufacturer's instructions.

APRIL

April is a glass of Champagne, ticklish and intoxicating. Cherry and pear trees shower us with soft pale petals and the hills turn a patchwork of pink and white and green. I decided to move home one April, visiting from tropical lands where I wearied of the light and bright colors that had once so attracted me. I yearned for gentle things. For puffy clouds, soft new grass, and squishy spring mud. For the sounds of the rain-filled creek behind our house. April is enchantment. A suspended state of disbelief that life could really be this grand, and a fervent prayer that it should always be so. In April we plant our seeds, as well as planting candy eggs and chocolates for little hands to harvest.

April is when asparagus starts to taste right, as do tender fresh peas, baby lettuces, and carrots. Perfect with simple roasts of chicken and lamb. Good enough to woo you home.

7.

Baby's Christening

My angel Moriah Vaughn was baptized in my family's church this spring. She was two and a half. I would have preferred to have done it sooner, but, as I am learning to expect from life, our christening was the more precious because of its late timing. Moriah will always remember the day that she walked with her family down the long, long aisle, holding her Mommy's hand. She'll remember our minister placing the water on her head as she looked with solemn, open eyes into the eyes of her greater family. After the service, our friends joined us in a party at home. We were blessed with one of those breezy, puffy clouded days, and a yard filled with beautiful, laughing children. My sisters and Mama brought much of the food, along with buckets of snowball blossoms from my parents' yard. I used Grandmama's old floral table cloths, and decorated platters with sage and chive blossoms from my courtyard garden.

This was my favorite party ever. My baby, my family, my friends, my God. An acknowledgement of blessing and responsibility. A celebration of our good fortune and of the privilege to serve.

The Menu

Poached Salmon

―――

Olive and Parsley Relish

―――

Dijon Sauce

―――

Mary's Asparagus

―――

Country Ham Salad

―――

Fresh Cheese Heart (Coeur à la Crème)

―――

Rhubarb and Ginger Chutney

―――

Baptism Cakes

―――

Quick-Pour Fondant Icing

Poached Salmon

Yes. I assume you know that salmon isn't a native of the American south. However, with the abundance of farm-raised salmon, it has become a staple which can be relied upon year round from almost any good grocer. I am spoiled. I have come to rely on the incredibly fresh salmon which my friend Kerim has air freighted into Nashville five days a week. He supplies the local sushi bars with salmon and most of their tuna. Need I say more.

Poached salmon is easy, and is perfect for satisfying a crowd with style. I break from the usual with a couple of different sauces I serve alongside. I would have just served my favorite: the olive and parsley relish, when I remembered that Godfather Sammy has an aversion to olives (poor man, he truly excels in countless other arenas). I quickly whipped up the dijon sauce out of scraps that are always in my fridge. Wouldn't you know it, most people preferred the dijon sauce.

A fish poacher is the right-sized pot for the job—custom designed. I believe they are worth the purchase if you poach even two of these a year. Poach the fish in the morning or the day ahead. If you like, you may save and even freeze the poaching liquid to use in soups and stews.

SERVES UP TO 20 IN A BUFFET-STYLE MEAL

1	side salmon, filleted and skinned (about 3 pounds)
2	cups dry white wine
	Juice of 2 lemons
3	sprigs parsley
2	scallions, cleaned
2	bay leaves
1	tablespoon salt
6	black peppercorns
½	teaspoon white pepper
½	teaspoon cayenne pepper
1½	teaspoons olive oil

Have your fish monger fillet the salmon, removing pin bones and skinning. Refrigerate covered until ready to poach. In the fish poacher on top of the rack combine the white wine, lemon juice, parsley, scallions, bay leaves, salt, peppercorns, white pepper, and cayenne pepper. Add enough water to take the liquid about half way up the sides of the poacher. Place the poacher on two burners on top of your stove and cover. Heat on high until boiling. Turn to medium and boil about 10 minutes more. Remove the cover. Turn the heat to low. Lay the fish on the rack outside of the poacher. Carefully lift the rack with the fish and place it into the simmering water. The water should almost cover the fish. Cover and cook on low for 9 minutes. After 9 minutes, turn off the heat, but keep the fish in the poacher with the lid closed for 9 more minutes. After 9 minutes, remove the cover and carefully lift the rack with the fish out of the liquid and rest it on a cookie sheet. Let cool, then cover lightly and refrigerate.

When you're ready to garnish the fish, use two spatulas to lift the fish onto your serving platter. Pour the olive oil over the fish and spread lightly with your fingers. This is mainly to make the fish look pretty and glistening. When it comes to garnish, I prefer a light hand. I literally throw a few chives and chive blossoms over mine. Dill is also pretty and considered classic with salmon. I add a few slim lemon circles and freshly cracked black pepper. Beautiful.

Place on a buffet with a meat or fish fork and knife. Serve with crackers or cocktail bread and the two sauces.

Olive and Parsley Relish

This is a great favorite of mine. I like to toss it with pasta, slather on summer corn, and spoon it into soups. Also quite nice on its own with some good crackers for cocktails.

MAKES 1 PINT

	About 18 oil-cured black olives
2	*cloves garlic, minced*
1	*bunch Italian parsley, roughly chopped*
1	*tablespoon capers, chopped*
¼	*cup olive oil*
	Zest and juice of 2 lemons
	Salt and cracked black pepper to taste

Use a small knife to cut the olives in half, removing the pit. Place the olive halves in a small mixing bowl with the remaining ingredients. Stir to mix. Refrigerate until 30 minutes before serving, at which time allow to come back to room temperature. Stir again and serve on the side with a small spoon.

Dijon Sauce

This is also quite nice with crudites such as blanched green beans, carrots, cauliflower, or asparagus.

If fresh tarragon isn't available, try finding a tarragon mustard to use for the dijon.

MAKES ABOUT 1 PINT

1	cup Hellman's mayonnaise (or homemade)
1½	tablespoons strong dijon mustard
½	cup heavy cream
1	teaspoon chopped fresh tarragon (optional)

In a medium bowl mix everything together. Refrigerate, covered, until ready to serve.

Mary's Asparagus

My sister's recipe. Great for picnics or to serve with cocktails—try sticking one in a Bloody Mary! No fat, either.

SERVES 4 TO 6

1	pound asparagus
⅓	cup tarragon wine vinegar
	Juice and grated zest from 1 lemon
1	teaspoon dijon mustard
2	scallions, thinly sliced
1	tablespoon chopped fresh parsley
	Freshly cracked black pepper to taste

Bring a large pot of salted water to a boil. Prepare a large bowl of ice water. Snap off the asparagus where the stalk becomes tender, about 3 inches from the base. Drop the asparagus into the boiling water and blanch for about 1 minute, until just cooked through. Drain and shock the asparagus in the ice water to stop the cooking. Mix together the remaining ingredients in a bowl large enough to hold the asparagus. Drain the asparagus and add to the marinade. Toss to coat. Let sit for 30 minutes before serving.

Country Ham Salad

This was Sallie's contribution to the party.

MAKES ABOUT 2 CUPS

¼	pound cooked country ham
2	tablespoons butter, softened
1	tablespoon dijon mustard
3	tablespoons mayonnaise
2	tablespoons pickle relish
1	tablespoon grated onion

In the bowl of a food processor fitted with a steel blade place the ham, butter, mustard, and mayonnaise, and process the mixture in pulses until it is fairly smooth, with a few lumps remaining. Add the relish and onion and pulse to combine. Taste and adjust seasoning. Serve in a bowl as a spread, or make individual tea sandwiches on rye bread.

Fresh Cheese Heart (Coeur à la Crème)

Most modern American recipes for this call for a mixture of cottage cheese and sour cream. Happily, real, fresh cheese is just recently more widely available. The closest source that I have is from Fromagerie Belle Chèvre, made in northern Alabama and sold in a couple of stores in Nashville. Times are definitely changing for the better when you can find national award winning cheeses like this outside of Manhattan or San Francisco. Scout around for yourselves. I bet there's an excellent fresh cheese made within one hundred miles of wherever you are.

Specialty cookware stores sell heart-shaped molds that have small holes for draining off the liquid from the cheese. You may choose to drain the cheese in a colander lined with cheesecloth, and then press the cheese into a mold or ramekin lined with plastic wrap.

SERVES ABOUT 20 FOR A BUFFET

2	*pounds fresh cheese (usually chèvre or goat cheese)*
1	*cup heavy cream*

In a mixing bowl mix together the cheese and cream. Line the coeur à la crème mold or the colander with cheesecloth and spoon the cheese mixture into this. Set over a pan with at least 1-inch sides. Let drain for 24 hours in the refrigerator. Unmold the cheese onto a serving tray, or spoon from the colander into a mold or ramekin lined with plastic wrap. Allow to set for 1 hour before unmolding onto serving tray.

Generously spoon chutney or marmalade over the cheese and serve with crackers or toast points.

Rhubarb and Ginger Chutney

Great with spring lamb, as well.

MAKES ABOUT 1 CUP

1	pound fresh rhubarb, diced
1	2-inch piece fresh ginger, peeled and grated
1	clove garlic, minced
½	red onion, diced
1	teaspoon red chile flakes
3	cardamom pods
1	tablespoon mustard seeds
¼	cup dried cranberries
1	cup firmly packed brown sugar
1½	cups white wine vinegar

In a non-corrosive saucepan combine everything. Bring to a boil, then reduce the heat to simmer. Simmer for 30 minutes until the rhubarb is softened and clear. Let cool.

Keeps covered in the refrigerator for 2 weeks or more.

Baptism Cakes

My mother made these beautiful little cakes, barely bigger than petits fours, iced in the palest green and pink, and decorated with tiny roses. They were precious. Moriah declared that she liked them even better than birthday cake.

This is a fairly complicated cake batter that I learned in culinary school. A simpler yellow or white cake recipe could be substituted.

MAKES ABOUT 24 SMALL CAKES

1½   cups sifted cake flour
¼   teaspoon salt
6   tablespoons butter, cut in bits
6   eggs
1   cup sugar
1   teaspoon vanilla extract
     Strawberry or seedless raspberry preserves
     Quick-Pour Fondant Icing *(recipe follows)*

Preheat the oven to 375°. Grease a jelly roll pan with shortening, then line with parchment or waxed paper. In a medium bowl sift together the flour and salt. In a saucepan melt the butter. Set aside. In the top of a double boiler whisk together the eggs and sugar. Set over simmering water (not touching the top pan) and stir until the mixture is hot to touch and no longer grainy. Don't heat too much or you will cook the eggs. Pour into the bowl of an electric mixer. Beat for about 4 minutes until it triples in volume and thickens. Add the vanilla and beat in. Fold in the flour in small batches with a rubber spatula. Fold about a cup of the batter into the butter, then fold this lightly back into the batter. Pour the batter into the prepared pan. Bake in the center of the oven for about 20 minutes until golden. Let cool in the pan for 5 minutes, then invert on a rack to cool.

To ice, cut the cake in half. Spread half with strawberry or seedless raspberry preserves. Top with the other half. Cut into squares and place the squares about ½ inch apart on a rack over waxed paper or parchment. Spoon Quick-Pour Fondant Icing over each.

Quick-Pour Fondant Icing

A true fondant is a tricky thing. This quick version suits fine for home cooks.

ENOUGH FOR 36 SMALL CAKES

6	*cups confectioners' sugar*
½	*cup water*
2	*tablespoons light corn syrup*
1	*teaspoon almond extract*
	Food coloring

Place the sugar in a heavy saucepan. Combine the water and the corn syrup and add to the sugar and mix well. Cook the icing over low heat, stirring, until it is smooth, shiny and somewhat thickened. Do not let the icing reach a temperature over 100°. Remove and stir in the food coloring.

My mother, "Child of the Depression" as she refers to herself, cannot bear the icing that gets wasted when you pour it over the cakes. She chooses to skewer the cakes on a toothpick or fork, and dip them into the icing. I myself am a spoiled product of the seventies. I pour.

8.

Soft Shell Season

I am mad about soft shell crabs. It is probably one of my baser, more primordial instincts, to devour large crustaceans whole, legs and all. I'll do it any time of year, but it's the middle of spring when I really get the urge. That's when they molt. Just like a snake loses its skin, a crab will lose its shell. I once worked with a chef from the bayou who told me of a magical time, I mean a period of a few hours, when the creatures first step out of their winter armor. There was a man living down the road from his restaurant who kept an eye on the crabs. The chef would get a hysterical call, during the middle of the dinner rush, "They're beautiful! I'm bringing them in." And so he would. In five gallon buckets, spidery legs in a mass of briny, tender flesh. I have come to know my darker side. It calls me when the soft shells come in.

The Menu

Deep-Fried Spicy Soft Shells

———

Sweet Potato and Beet Chips

———

Crunchy Cole Slaw

———

Frozen Strawberry Yogurt

Deep-Fried Spicy Soft Shells

A good way to eat most anything.

SERVES 6 HUNGRY CRAB EATERS

12	soft shell crabs
2	cups buttermilk
	Several squirts Crystal hot sauce
	Juice of 2 lemons
1	cup self-rising flour
1	cup cornmeal
	Salt and pepper
	Oil for frying

Clean the soft shells by removing the eyes and the dead men—that is, the gills underneath the shell, so called because they can choke you—or, have your fish monger do this. Place them in a bowl with the buttermilk, hot sauce, and lemon juice. Turn them to coat well, cover, and let marinate in the refrigerator for at least 30 minutes and up to a few hours.

In a shallow dish mix together the flour, cornmeal, salt, and pepper. Dredge the softshells in the flour mixture, then refrigerate for about 1 hour.

In a deep-fryer or very heavy saucepan heat several inches of oil. The oil should be about 350°. You don't want it smoking. Fry the soft shells a couple at a time for about 5 minutes until crispy and golden brown. Drain on clean brown paper bags. Serve at once with lots of lemon and hot sauce, or with remoulade.

Sweet Potato and Beet Chips

I'm afraid these are addictive. Deep-fry the chips before the soft shells. You can use the same oil.

SERVES 6

2   medium sweet potatoes
2   medium beets
    Oil for frying
    Salt

Peel the sweet potatoes and beets. If you have a mandolin or commercial slicer, you can make really thin chips. If not, you can try using a peeler, or just slice them with a knife as thinly as you can. Place them on several layers of paper towels and sprinkle salt over them. Let sit for about 30 minutes, then blot them as dryly as you can. Meanwhile, heat the oil to about 325°. Fry the chips in small batches until crispy and beginning to brown. Drain on clean brown paper bags and sprinkle with salt. Serve hot or room temp (they'll start to get soft soon, so eat them fast!).

Crunchy Cole Slaw

The raw turnip gives it the extra crunch.

SERVES 6

¼	head green cabbage, thinly sliced
¼	head purple cabbage, thinly sliced
1	turnip, peeled and cut in match sticks
½	red onion, cut in thin slices
1	carrot, peeled and cut in match sticks
3	tablespoons mayonnaise
2	teaspoons dijon mustard
	Juice of 2 lemons
	Salt and pepper

In a large bowl mix everything together. Season to taste and serve.

Frozen Strawberry Yogurt

April is still early for local berries, so I sometimes cheat and use California driscolls.

MAKES ABOUT 1 QUART

1	quart strawberries, stemmed
1/3	cup honey
1	pint plain low-fat yogurt
	Juice from 1 lemon
1/2	teaspoon rose water (optional)

Place the strawberries and honey in the bowl of a food processor fitted with a metal blade and process until puréed. Pour into a mixing bowl and stir in the yogurt, lemon juice, and rose water if desired. Freeze in an ice cream maker according to the manufacturer's instructions.

9.

A Tea Party for Mommies and Their Girls

I revel in being the Mommy of a little girl. You get to do all of that neat stuff all over again! Dolls and dress up. Horses and fairy Godmothers and Happily Ever After. I don't know why we ever give it up in the first place.

At our home, we are particularly fond of tea parties. We make fancy food and dress up quite smart. Sometimes we invite Nana. Sometimes it's only Baby Kitty Cat and us. This tea party is very special—for other mommies and their little girls and dollies. The girls feel so grown up, and the mommies get to chat and admire their babies. Tea parties in the nursery are fun, but the best ones are out of doors, on lawns or patios, with big hats on little girls and their dolls.

The Menu

Lemon Poppy Seed Pound Cake

———

Watercress Sandwiches

———

Radish Tea Sandwiches

———

Tuna Salad Puffs

———

Cheese Scones with Country Ham

———

Lavender Scented Shortbread

Lemon Poppy Seed Pound Cake

One of my all time favorites.

MAKES 1 9-INCH LOAF

3	cups all-purpose flour
1	teaspoon baking powder
½	teaspoon salt
1	cup (2 sticks) butter, softened
1¾	cups sugar
8	eggs, separated
	Juice and grated zest of 1 lemon
2	tablespoons poppy seeds

Preheat the oven to 350°. Grease and flour a 9-inch loaf pan. In a medium bowl sift together the flour, baking powder, and salt. Set aside.

In a large bowl cream the butter until fluffy, then beat in ¾ cup of the sugar. Beat in the egg yolks, then the lemon juice and zest and poppy seeds. Gradually fold in the flour.

In a separate bowl beat the egg whites to soft peak. Sprinkle over the remaining cup of sugar, then beat to stiff peaks. Gently fold the egg whites into the mixture. Pour into the prepared pan and bake in the center of the oven for 1 hour or until a cake tester inserted in the center comes out clean. Let cool in the pan for 15 minutes. Turn out onto a rack and cool completely. Slice thinly for tea.

Watercress Sandwiches

Watercress grows wild in our creeks throughout the spring. It's usually available in groceries, as well.

MAKES 12 OPEN-FACE TEA SANDWICHES

1	8-ounce package cream cheese or soft goat cheese, softened
1	bunch watercress, finely chopped
6	thin slices bread, white or whole wheat
	Zest of 2 lemons

In a medium bowl mix the cream cheese with the watercress. Spread evenly over each slice of bread. Use a biscuit cutter to cut out 2 tea sandwiches about 2 inches in diameter, from each slice. Use a zester to remove the lemon zest. Garnish each tea sandwich with a bit of the zest and serve.

Radish Tea Sandwiches

MAKES 12 TEA SANDWICHES

½ cup (1 stick) unsalted butter, softened
1 tablespoon chopped parsley
   Salt and cracked black pepper to taste
1 bunch radishes, cleaned and cut in thin circles
   Thinly sliced white or rye bread

In a medium bowl mix the butter with the parsley. Spread evenly over each bread slice. Cut the bread into tea-sized pieces and top with overlapping slices of radish. Sprinkle with salt, cracked black pepper, and additional parsley, and serve.

Tuna Salad Puffs

I love tuna salad. This one is very mild.

MAKES 12 PUFFS

FOR THE PASTRY PUFFS:

½   cup all-purpose flour

¼   cup water

¼   cup milk

¼   cup (½ stick) butter, cut in small pieces

¼   teaspoon salt

2   large eggs

FOR THE SALAD:

2   6-ounce cans solid albacore tuna

1   stick celery, finely chopped

2   scallions, sliced thinly

1   carrot, grated roughly

¼   cup Hellman's mayonnaise (or homemade)

¼   cup slivered almonds

1   teaspoon minced fresh dill

Line a baking pan with parchment or waxed paper. Preheat the oven to 400°.

Sift the flour and set aside. In a heavy saucepan combine the water, milk, butter and salt. Bring to a full boil, then add the flour all at once. Stir with a wooden spoon until the mixture pulls away from the sides of the pan. Remove from the heat and beat in one egg, and then the other. Beat the dough until it is smooth and shiny.

Spoon the dough in heaping tablespoons onto the prepared pan. Bake for 15 minutes. Turn oven down to 350° and bake for about 20 more minutes. Turn off the oven.

Poke a hole in each puff and let cool in the oven for 10 minutes. Remove and let dry completely. Makes about 15 puffs

Drain the tuna very well. Break up the tuna with a fork. In a medium bowl mix the tuna with the remaining ingredients. Cut the top off each puff. Spoon the salad into the puffs. Place the lids on top and serve.

Cheese Scones with Country Ham

Rich cheese scones work well with the bite of country ham.

MAKES 12 SMALL SCONES

2	cups all-purpose flour
1	tablespoon baking powder
1/2	teaspoon salt
1	cup grated sharp Cheddar cheese
1 1/4	cups plus 3 teaspoons cream
1/4	cup (1/2 stick) butter, softened
1/2	pound thinly sliced country ham

Preheat the oven to 425°. In a large bowl mix together the flour, baking powder, and salt. Stir in the cheese. Stir in 1 1/4 cups of cream, mixing to make a soft dough. Gather together and knead gently in the bowl, gathering all of the loose dough. Transfer to a floured surface. Pat out to a 3/4-inch thick rectangle. Cut the dough into 12 wedges or triangles. Space 1/2 inch apart on an ungreased baking sheet. Brush the tops with cream. Bake for about 15 minutes until golden brown.

Let cool. Split and spread with a bit of soft butter. Stuff with very thin slices of country ham and serve.

Lavender-Scented Shortbread

My lavender starts blooming in April. I like to roast chicken with lavender blossoms set in the cavity to scent the whole bird. The flavor and aroma are intriguing in this simple shortbread, as well.

MAKES ABOUT 24 BARS

½	cup plus 2 tablespoons (1¼ sticks) unsalted butter
¼	cup confectioners' sugar
1½	teaspoons sugar
¼	teaspoon salt
1½	cups all-purpose flour
1	tablespoon fresh lavender blossoms, broken apart (or 1 teaspoon dried)

Preheat the oven to 300°. In a large bowl beat the butter, sugars, and salt until light and fluffy. Gradually mix in the flour and then the lavender. Press the dough into an 8-inch square baking pan and even out the top. Bake about 45 minutes or until just beginning to turn golden.

Let cool in the pan, but cut into bars while the shortbread is still warm.

10.

Easter Dinner

*E*aster is my favorite of the traditional holidays. My mother would say that this is the good Christian in me—Easter is, after all, the foundation of our faith.

Of course. But I am additionally drawn to the pastel colors and creativity of egg decorating, and I relish the time spent outdoors hiding and hunting eggs in the lamb-like days of spring. Plus, I'm a sucker for a child suitably festooned for the occasion. Now I get to admire my own daughter, quite proud of herself in her Easter best. It's like falling in love again.

I'm a bit weepy-eyed in church throughout the processional and first hymn. It started when I was twenty-two, the first year a ceremonial cross was marched down the center aisle in memory of a friend we had lost far too young. That day I clutched my mother's hand for strength, and now I grasp Moriah's as well. Today marks springtime, rebirth, and faith. Today is a holy day.

We celebrate holy days with feasts, as all cultures have for all time. Easter foods are full of promise, tender and precious.

The Menu

Roasted Free Range Hen

———

Spring Peas with Mint and Scallions

———

Stuffed Eggs with Caviar

———

Lemon-Scented Yeast Rolls

———

Steamed New Potatoes with Butter and Garlic

———

Coconut Lamb Cake

Roasted Free Range Hen

There's nothing better than the simplicity of a well roasted chicken. Free range hens definitely have more flavor, and there are even some available that are organic.

SERVES 8

4	carrots, peeled
3	stalks celery
2	white or yellow onions
2	large free range hens
3	cloves garlic
2	teaspoons salt
½	teaspoon black pepper
8	sprigs fresh thyme (or 1 teaspoon dried)
1	lemon
¼	cup olive oil

Preheat the oven to 425°. Rinse the carrot and celery and roughly chop, along with the onions. Place all in the bottom of the roasting pan. Remove the giblets from the hens and discard or reserve for another use. Rinse the hens well and pat dry. Peel and thinly slice the garlic. On the cutting board, sprinkle the salt and pepper over the garlic. Mince with a knife until you have a paste. Work this paste under the skin of the chicken on the breasts and thighs. Push the thyme under the skin, as well. Cut the lemon in half and place one half in the cavity of each chicken. Dribble the oil over the chickens and sprinkle with additional salt and pepper, if desired. Arrange the chickens over the vegetables, breast-side down. Place in the oven and roast for about 30 minutes.

Turn the chickens over, turn the oven down to 350°, and roast about 40 more minutes until done.

Remove from the oven and let rest about 5 or 10 minutes. Take the chickens to a cutting board and cut in quarters, or remove from the bone and slice. Arrange on a platter with the roast vegetables. Pour the pan juices over all and serve.

Spring Peas with Mint and Scallions

I know that fresh peas are difficult to find. You may substitute frozen, but the taste won't be the same. Ask your grocer about fresh. The more people that do, the more likely that fresh peas, once a springtime mainstay, will show up again at the market.

SERVES 8

4	cups fresh shelled peas
¼	cup (½ stick) butter
¼	cup roughly chopped fresh mint
3	scallions, sliced thinly
	Salt and white pepper to taste

Bring a pot of salted water to a boil. Add the peas and cook about 5 minutes until tender. Drain the peas and toss in a bowl with the remaining ingredients. Serve warm.

Stuffed Eggs with Caviar

While caviar has traditionally come from Eastern Europe and Asia, the last decade has seen the industry develop in Tennessee, Kentucky, and Georgia. The caviar is excellent: fresh tasting like the sea.

Caviar is such a treat, I generally use it sparingly. Stuffed eggs are the perfect vehicle. If you make your eggs ahead of time, don't garnish with the caviar until you're ready to serve them, so that the caviar doesn't run or "bleed."

MAKES 16 STUFFED HALVES

8	eggs
1½	tablespoons mayonnaise
1	teaspoon dijon mustard
1	teaspoon fresh dill
	Salt and cayenne pepper to taste
1	ounce caviar

Place the eggs in a pot and cover with water. Bring the water to a boil and let boil for 10 minutes.

Place the eggs in a bowl of ice water and let cool about 5 minutes. The ice water should make the eggs pull back from the shell, making them easier to peel. Peel the eggs carefully, slice in half lengthwise, then place the yolks in a small mixing bowl. Add the mayonnaise, mustard, dill, salt, and cayenne, and mash with a fork. Spoon a heaping teaspoon back into each egg white and garnish with a small bit of the caviar. Refrigerate until ready to serve.

Lemon-Scented Yeast Rolls

Just the hint of lemon.

1	package active dry yeast
3	tablespoons warm water
1	cup warm milk
5	tablespoons butter, melted
2	tablespoons sugar
1	egg, lightly beaten
1	teaspoon salt
	Grated zest of 1 lemon
2	cups bread flour
1½	cups all-purpose flour, or as needed
2	teaspoons vegetable oil

In a large bowl combine the yeast and water. Let stand for 5 minutes, until the yeast has dissolved. Mix in the milk, butter, sugar, egg, salt, and lemon zest. Gradually stir in the bread flour and then the all-purpose flour. If the dough is too sticky, you may add up to ½ cup more all-purpose flour. Knead the dough for about 10 minutes, either by hand or with a dough hook in a mixer.

Pour the oil in a mixing bowl. Add the dough, turning it to coat with the oil. Cover the dough and set in a warm spot to rise. Let the dough rise about 1 hour to 1 hour and 30 minutes, until doubled in size.

Punch the dough down and knead a few moments. Place back in the bowl, cover, and refrigerate for 30 minutes. Remove the dough and divide into 24 pieces. Roll them into balls, cover and let rest for 10 minutes. Flatten the balls into ovals. Brush these with melted butter, then fold one half over the other. Place on a greased baking pan, cover lightly and let rise about an hour, until doubled.

cream the butter. Add the eggs one at a time, beating after each addition. Beat for about 3 minutes until light. Stir in half the dry mixture, then half of the sour cream. Repeat. Stir in the flavorings and zest, and pour into the prepared pan. Bake for 1 hour to 1 hour and 15 minutes until a cake tester inserted in the center comes out clean. Allow to cool in the pan before turning out and frosting.

For the frosting, in a large saucepan bring the water to a boil on top of the stove. Add 2 cups of the sugar and corn syrup. Bring back to a boil and continue to boil until the mixture reaches 238°.

In the meantime, beat the whites until foamy. Add ¼ cup of sugar and beat to a stiff peak. When the syrup has reached the proper temperature, pour it into the egg whites in a slow, steady stream, beating like mad the whole time. Add the vanilla and blend well. Let the icing cool before frosting the cake. Garnish with lots of freshly grated coconut.

II.

Faeryland Picnic

The hills behind my parents' house, part of the Radnor Lake Preserve, become enchanted each spring, with a carpet of pale pink spring beauties, and white wind flowers with their kelly green foliage. There are patches of blue bells and banks by the creek strewn with trout lilies. The trilliums and jack-in-the-pulpits are houses for the woods sprites, and the Solomon's seal their staff of tiny bells. During this time we call the valley Faeryland. It's before-the-snakes-are-really-out time, the time for picnics on faded quilts, and salamander hunts in the chilly creek. When we were young, my mother was wonderful for packing us up and herding us deep into the heart of Faeryland to sojourn amongst the fancies of wood nymphs and sprites. These are magic days of clearest blue sky framed in pink and black against the redbud trees. These are days to relish with family and friends and God's good land.

The Menu

Strawberry Bread

———

Cracked Pepper Cream Cheese

———

Picnic Thighs

———

Cracked Wheat Salad with Turnips, Carrots, and Dill

———

Dressed Sugar Snaps

———

Pansy Cookies

Strawberry Bread

An easy quick bread using fresh berries.

MAKES 1 LOAF

1	quart fresh strawberries
2	cups sugar
4	eggs
3	cups all-purpose flour
1	teaspoon salt
1	teaspoon baking soda
1	teaspoon ground cinnamon
1¼	cups vegetable oil
1½	cups almond slices
¼	cup chopped fresh mint (optional)

Preheat the oven to 350°. Grease and flour 2 standard loaf pans.

Mash the strawberries with 1 cup of the sugar. Set aside. Beat the eggs with the remaining cup of sugar. Set aside. In a large bowl sift the dry ingredients. Mix in the egg mixture and stir in the strawberries and the oil. Pour into the prepared loaf pans. Bake in the center of the oven for 1 hour. Let cool completely before turning out.

Cracked Pepper Cream Cheese

You may leave out the pepper, if you are picnicking with little ones who have delicate palates.

FOR 1 CUP

1	8-ounce package cream cheese
1	teaspoon fresh lemon juice
½	teaspoon freshly cracked black pepper

Let the cheese sit out to soften. In a mixing bowl stir together all the ingredients. Keeps covered in the refrigerator for a week. Let come to room temperature before spreading.

For the sandwiches: Slice the strawberry bread about ½ inch thick. You may use a flower or heart shaped cookie cutter to make the sandwiches even more festive. Spread half the slices with the cheese. Top with the remaining slices and serve.

Picnic Thighs

This was Sallie's idea, years ago. The thighs get so tender, the meat simply melts off the bone.

SERVES 6 TO 8

12	bone-in, skin-on chicken thighs
1	tablespoon olive oil
2	cloves garlic, pushed through a press
2	teaspoons fresh thyme leaves (or ½ teaspoon dried)
1	teaspoon fresh marjoram leaves (or ½ teaspoon dried)

Preheat the oven to 325°. Rinse the thighs, pat dry, and place in a baking dish. Mix together the remaining ingredients. Coat the thighs with the marinade, pushing some up under the skin. Bake the thighs, covered, for 1 hour.

Let cool and serve at room temperature.

Cracked Wheat Salad with Turnips, Carrots, and Dill

Cracked wheat, or bulgur, is usually associated with Middle Eastern foods, but is now widely available.

SERVES 6

3	cups boiling water
1	cup medium cracked wheat
1	medium white or yellow turnip, peeled
1	medium carrot, peeled
1	bunch fresh dill, chopped
1	bunch fresh parsley, chopped
	Juice of 1 lemon
1	tablespoon olive oil
1	teaspoon salt
	Black pepper to taste

In a large bowl pour the boiling water over the cracked wheat. Soak about 10 minutes, until just tender. Pour off any remaining water. Coarsely grate the turnip and carrot and add to the cracked wheat, along with the remaining ingredients. Toss, taste, and adjust seasonings. Serve room temp.

Dressed Sugar Snaps

The crunchy sugar snap is sweet enough to eat raw. I just dress it up a bit.

SERVES 6

1	pound fresh sugar snap peas
1	shallot, minced
2	tablespoons olive oil
1	tablespoon champagne or white wine vinegar
1	tablespoon chopped fresh parsley

Rinse and string the sugar snaps. Blanche in boiling, salted water about 30 seconds. Drain and cool immediately under cold running water or in an ice water bath. Drain thoroughly and toss in a bowl with the remaining ingredients. Serve room temperature.

Pansy Cookies

Fresh pansies baked right on top make these cookies extra special. Be sure you gather your flowers from a spot that's pesticide free.

MAKES ABOUT 4 DOZEN COOKIES

1	cup (2 sticks) butter
1	cup sugar
2	eggs
2	teaspoons baking soda
2	tablespoons milk
2	teaspoons vanilla extract
2	teaspoons cream of tartar
3½	cups all-purpose flour
	Pinch of salt
2	egg whites
	Clean pansies blossoms
½	cup sanding sugar

In a large bowl cream the butter and sugar. Mix in the eggs. Dissolve the baking soda in the milk and add, along with the vanilla, to the creamed mixture. In a separate bowl sift the dry ingredients together, and stir into the creamed mixture. Mix thoroughly. Gather the dough into a ball and wrap in plastic wrap. Chill for 15 minutes.

Preheat the oven to 325°. On a floured surface roll out the dough to ¼-inch thickness and cut out plain or fluted circles. Bake on an ungreased cookie sheet for about 5 minutes. Remove from the oven and brush the tops of the cookies with the egg whites. Place one pansy on top, spreading out the petals and topping with a bit more egg white. Sprinkle with sanding sugar. Bake for another 5 minutes until they just start to brown. Cool and store in one layer in an airtight container.

MAY

May is full of herself, laughing, as are we. Catching our stride as though youth and spring will never end. Picnics and horse races, celebrations abound. Suitable occasions for ladies in hats. Days lengthen and the earth grows warm. School is almost out. May is time for serious play. The flowers are glorious—peonies as big as your hand and iris in their regal stance. Magnolias start to bloom, filling whole blocks with their remarkable scent as graduates strut about, brimming with importance.

It's time to clean the grill. Hose down patio chairs and clean off the table. You may see a tomato at the market. Don't trust it. It's still not time. Enjoy the asparagus and sugar snap peas, crisp cress from the still-cool creeks and sweet Vidalia onions. Don't yearn too much for home-grown berries. Remember, when they come in, it's almost time to wave good-bye to spring.

12.

Engagement Party

*T*his party is an intimate festivity for close friends. Recently I have seen a flurry of engagements and unions. Many of my friends in their thirties and forties seem to be finally settling down. And while some have made earlier commitments that didn't quite work, I am happy to note a pleasing sense of groundedness, a decisiveness in their nature as well as mine.

It's difficult to avoid the anxieties and complexities associated with weddings, no matter the maturity of the couple or the size of the affair. A cozy evening with a few select guests is a marvelous gift for an otherwise harried couple. It gives them a chance to slow down and be pampered by true friends who want to share in memories that will last long after the "Big Day."

This is a lovely meal, full of vivid sensations. Enjoy it out of doors, if the weather permits, or in a snug spot by the fire.

The Menu

Seared Shrimp with Blood Oranges

———

Parmesan Mayonnaise Muffins

———

Dijon and Almond-Coated Lamb Chops

———

Buttermilk Blue Cheese Grits

———

Sautéed Spinach

———

Raspberry Sherbet

———

Walnut Biscuits

Radish Tea Sandwiches (page 95)

Roasted Free Range Hen and Spring Peas with Mint and Scallions (page 101)

Pansy Cookies (page 116)

Raspberry Sherbet (page 134)

Roast Pork Loin and Vidalia Onion Marmalade on Herbed Yeast Rolls (page 139)

Vidalia Onion Pizza with Country Ham (page 146)

Rhubarb and Ginger Pie (page 159)

Grilled Veal Chops with Shiitakes and Mint and Orange Relish (page 163)

Dijon and Almond-Coated Lamb Chops

The almonds make a great, crispy crust.

SERVES 6

12	lamb chops
	Salt and pepper
2	tablespoons dijon mustard
½	cup blanched almonds
¼	cup bread crumbs
2	cloves garlic
1	tablespoon chopped fresh parsley
	Fresh ground black pepper

Rinse the lamb chops and pat dry. Season with salt and pepper. Rub the dijon over the cut sides of the lamb chops.

In a shallow bowl mix together the remaining ingredients.

Dredge the chops in the almond mixture. Preheat the oven to 400°, while you refrigerate the chops for 30 minutes.

Bake the chops on a non-stick baking pan for about 6 minutes per side, turning once for rare to medium rare. Remove from the oven and serve.

Buttermilk Blue Cheese Grits

Unabashedly rich.

SERVES 6

---

2   cups buttermilk
2   cups sweet milk
1   cup grits, preferably stone-ground
6   ounces crumbled blue cheese
     Salt and pepper to taste

Preheat the oven to 375°. In a saucepan heat the buttermilk and milk milk and stir in the grits. (The buttermilk will curdle. Don't worry, the texture will be fine once it bakes.) Cook, stirring occasionally, for about 10 minutes until thickened and creamy. Remove from the heat and stir in the blue cheese. Season to taste and let cool slightly.

Beat the eggs and stir into the grits. Bake for 20 minutes until puffed and slightly browned.

Sautéed Spinach

SERVES 6

2   pounds spinach
3   tablespoons olive oil
½   red onion, thinly sliced
1   clove garlic, minced
     Juice of 1 lemon
     Salt and pepper

Clean the spinach well and drain. In a deep skillet heat the oil. Add the onion and cook on high about 2 minutes. Add the spinach. It may be appear to be too much for the pan, but it will cook down quickly. Sprinkle the garlic over the spinach. Cover for about 30 seconds, just long enough for it to wilt. Add the lemon juice, salt, and pepper. Toss, taste, and adjust the seasoning. Serve.

Raspberry Sherbet

SERVES 6

2 cups sugar
1 cup cream
3 pints fresh raspberries
Juice of 1 lemon

In a small pot mix the cream and sugar. Bring to a simmer and cook for 5 minutes. Let cool. In a blender purée the raspberries and lemon juice. Strain out the seeds. Blend in the cream. Refrigerate for 1 hour.

Pour into an ice cream maker and freeze according to the manufacturer's instructions.

Walnut Biscuits

These are also very nice for tea with cheese. Just sweet enough.

MAKES 18 BISCUITS

1	cup all-purpose flour
½	cup firmly packed brown sugar
1	cup finely ground walnuts
¼	cup (½ stick) butter, cut into bits

Grease a baking sheet. Preheat the oven to 400°.

In a bowl mix together the flour, brown sugar, and walnuts. Use a pastry knife to cut in the butter. Blend briefly by hand to form a dough. On a floured surface, pat the dough out ¼-inch thick. Use a heart shaped cookie cutter to cut out the biscuits. Transfer to a baking sheet and bake for 15 minutes until the edges begin to brown slightly. Let cool on the pan.

Pass on a tray, or tuck one or two biscuits into each glass of sherbet to serve.

13.

Steeplechase Boxes

Steeplechase is Nashville's answer to Ascot. The hallowed event takes place on what is usually one of the most beautiful weekends of the year, in early May. This is a serious equestrian event, with riders and spectators from Europe and all around the country. Besides the horses and riders, the most important matters of the day are as follows: A) What one is wearing. B) What one is eating.

West Nashville's toniest caterers and take out establishments jockey as competitively as the riders, so as to have their logos conspicuously placed on the greatest number of picnic packages in the prestigious box seats. The truly savvy box holder side steps the masses with unique creations of their own invention.

As a former west Nashville caterer myself, with years of experience in facing the challenges of heat, rain, and bumpy transportation, I can confidently state that this box lunch works, scrumptiously so. I say outdo the others and do it yourself.

The Menu

Roast Pork Loin

———

Lemon and Vidalia Onion Marmalade

———

Herbed Yeast Rolls

———

Roasted Asparagus

———

Wild Rice Salad with Currants and Almonds

———

Chocolate Bourbon Chess Tarts

Roast Pork Loin

Moist and flavorful. I prefer it to beef.

SERVES 6

1	*2-pound pork loin, rinsed and trimmed*
1	*tablespoon garlic salt*
2	*teaspoons black pepper*
2	*tablespoons olive oil*

Place the pork loin in a bowl. Add the remaining ingredients and rub them into the pork loin. Cover and refrigerate at least 30 minutes.

Preheat the oven to 400°. Let the loin set out of the refrigerator for 5 or 10 minutes before roasting. Place the loin on an oiled rack over a roasting pan. Roast about 30 minutes, until the pork is medium, about 145° in the center. Don't overcook, or the meat will dry out.

Let the meat rest a good 10 minutes before slicing about ½ inch thick. Refrigerate until you assemble the rolls.

Lemon and Vidalia Onion Marmalade

Try it also with grilled fish or chicken.

MAKES ABOUT I PINT

3	lemons
4	Vidalia onions, cut lengthwise in thin slices
⅓	cup white wine
⅓	cup white wine vinegar
¼	cup firmly packed brown sugar
¼	cup honey
1	teaspoon minced fresh sage

Use a vegetable peeler to remove the zest from the lemons in wide strips. Reserve the zested lemons. Cut the strips of zest width-wise into small pieces. In a medium non-corrosive pot on top of the stove combine the lemon zest, onions, wine, vinegar, brown sugar, and honey. Cook over low heat, stirring, until the sugar has dissolved. Add the sage, stir, and simmer the mixture about 30 minutes. Stir in the juice from one or two of the lemons (taste for tartness) and cook until the juice is absorbed. Let cool and refrigerate, covered, until ready to use, up to 3 weeks.

Herbed Yeast Rolls

MAKES ABOUT 12 LARGE ROLLS

Follow the recipe for Lemon Scented Yeast Rolls (p. 104), substituting 1 tablespoon of minced fresh parsley for the lemon zest. Divide the dough into 12 portions.

To assemble, allow the rolls to cool. Stuff with sliced pork and a good dollop of marmalade. Serve room temperature.

Roasted Asparagus

Roasting develops the delicate flavor. Less messy to eat than marinated asparagus.

SERVES 8

2   bunches fresh asparagus
2   tablespoons olive oil
     Salt and pepper
2   scallions, thinly sliced
1   teaspoon toasted sesame seeds

Preheat the oven to 425°. Break off the tough portion of the asparagus and discard. Rinse and pat dry the asparagus and place on a baking sheet. Pour the oil over and sprinkle with salt and pepper. Toss to coat evenly. Roast the asparagus until just tender and slightly browned, about 10 minutes.

Meanwhile, place the scallions in a bowl along with the sesame seeds. Toss the roasted asparagus in the bowl and mix gently. Let cool. Serve room temperature.

Wild Rice Salad with Currants and Almonds

This is good warm, as well.

Serves 8

1	cup medium or long grain rice
	Salt
2	tablespoons butter
1	cup wild rice
2	tablespoons currants
1	tablespoon champagne or white wine vinegar
½	red onion, diced
1	stick celery, diced
3	scallions, thinly sliced
½	cup sliced almonds, toasted
2	teaspoons minced fresh tarragon (or parsley)
	Juice and zest of 1 orange
2	tablespoons olive oil
	Salt and pepper to taste

Cook the two kinds of rice separately. For the white rice, in a pot bring 2 cups water to a boil with 1 teaspoon of salt and 1 tablespoon of butter. Add the rice, stir, and bring back to a boil. Stir again, cover, and simmer for 15 minutes until the rice is tender and all of the water is absorbed. Remove from the heat and toss with a fork.

For the wild rice, in a pot bring 3 cups of water to a boil with 1 teaspoon of salt and 1 tablespoon of butter. Add the rice, stir, and bring back to a boil. Reduce the heat and simmer about 30 minutes until cooked. Drain and let cool.

Meanwhile, in a large bowl soak the currants in the vinegar. Add the cooled rice and remaining ingredients. Stir and taste for seasoning. Serve at room temperature.

Chocolate Bourbon Chess Tarts

A classic southern dessert for a classic event.

MAKES 8 TARTS

1	recipe pie crust
1½	squares unsweetened chocolate
½	cup (1 stick) butter
1	tablespoon all-purpose flour
1	cup firmly packed brown sugar
½	cup sugar
2	eggs, beaten lightly
1	tablespoon milk
1	tablespoon good bourbon

Grease 8 tart pans. Roll out the pastry to about ⅛ inch thick. Cut circles about 2 inches wider than your tart pans. Pat the dough into the pans and crimp the edges with a fork. Refrigerate while you prepare the filling.

Preheat the oven to 350°. In the top of a double boiler melt the chocolate and butter, stirring until smooth. In a bowl mix together the flour and sugars, and add to the butter and chocolate. Mix well. In a small bowl beat the eggs with the milk and bourbon. Add to the batter and beat by hand until smooth. Pour into the prepared tart pans. Brush the rim of the crust with a little beaten egg. Bake the tarts for about 20 minutes.

Let cool and serve room temperature.

14.

Pizza Down Here

This meal is for my daughter, Moriah. Try telling her that pizza is not indigenous to the South. It is to hers. She adores pizza, probably because we don't have it very often. I've always let her help me roll out the crust and arrange the toppings.

We grow lots of lettuce in the spring, and gathering the leaves is Moriah's special job. She even picks the thyme for the dressing (with a little help). We like to make this especially on Saturday, when we watch movies together. We spread a blanket on the floor in the den and have a picnic before the television. When it's warm, we pause our show and enjoy the raspberries outside. Raspberries in the den still make me a bit anxious.

I've tried to legitimize the inclusion of pizza in a southern text by offering cornmeal, Vidalias, and country ham. Purists may not be placated. So be it.

The Menu

Vidalia Onion Pizza with Country Ham

———

Spring Salad with Honey Lemon Thyme Vinaigrette

———

Fresh Raspberries with Crème Fraîche

Vidalia Onion Pizza with Country Ham

The cornmeal in the dough makes this crust crispy and delicious. Vidalia onions come in season mid-spring. Their natural flavor is a sweet contrast to the salty country ham.

SERVES 6

1	recipe cornmeal pizza dough
¼	cup Green Pesto (recipe follows)
1	Vidalia onion
4	ounces cooked country ham, sliced very thinly
4	ounces fresh goat cheese

FOR THE PIZZA DOUGH:

½	teaspoon sugar
¾	cup warm (100°) water
1¼	teaspoons active dry yeast (a little over ½ an envelope)
¼	cup cornmeal
1½	cups or more all-purpose flour
½	teaspoon salt
1	teaspoon olive oil

For the dough, place the sugar in a bowl and pour the water over, stirring to dissolve. Sprinkle the yeast over the sugar water and whisk in. Set aside until the top is foamy. If it doesn't foam, discard and start again. Your water was either too hot or too cold (it should be just over body temperature), or your yeast was too old.

Meanwhile, sift the cornmeal, flour, and salt into a bowl and form a well in the center. Add the foamy yeast mixture and the olive oil and mix until a soft dough forms. If it's too sticky, add a little extra flour. Turn out on a floured surface and knead about 5 minutes. Place in an oiled bowl, turning to coat. Cover loosely with plastic and set in a warm place to rise until doubled in volume, about 1 hour.

Preheat the oven to 475°. Grease a baking sheet and dust with cornmeal. Punch down the dough, roll into a ball, and let rest about 10 minutes while you assemble the toppings.

Flatten the dough on a floured surface and roll in a $\frac{1}{4}$-inch thick circle, about 12 inches in diameter. Brush lightly with olive oil and use your fingers to make small dents in the crust.

Lightly spread on the pesto. Scatter the onion circles and country ham. Top with small blobs of goat cheese. Bake about 20 minutes until the dough is cooked through and the top is lightly browned and bubbly. Serve at once.

Green Pesto

A wonderfully clean and bright flavor.

MAKES ABOUT 2 CUPS

½	cup fresh parsley leaves
½	cup fresh mint leaves
½	cup fresh dill
½	cup toasted pecans
3	cloves garlic
¾	cup olive oil
	Juice and zest of 1 lemon
	Salt and freshly ground black pepper to taste

In the bowl of a food processor fitted with a metal blade place the herb leaves, garlic, and pecans. With the motor running, pour the oil slowly through the feed tube, forming a slightly chunky paste. Remove the lid and stir in the lemon juice, salt, and pepper to taste. Keeps two to three days covered in the refrigerator, or may be frozen.

This may also be used as a pasta sauce, a sauce for chicken, fish or pork, or simply spread on sandwiches.

Spring Salad with Honey Lemon Thyme Vinaigrette

The honey makes this just sweet enough.

SERVES 6

FOR THE SALAD:

2 heads Bibb or Boston lettuce
1 head radicchio

FOR THE VINAIGRETTE:

   Juice and zest of 2 lemons
¼ cup honey
2 tablespoons champagne or white wine vinegar
1 teaspoon fresh thyme leaves
½ cup olive oil
   Salt and white pepper to taste

Remove the core from the lettuce and separate the leaves. Lightly rinse (the tender leaves bruise easily) and spin dry. Cut the radicchio in half, remove the core, and thinly slice. Toss with the lettuce, cover with a paper towel, and refrigerate until just prior to serving. Toss with vinaigrette and serve.

For the vinaigrette, in a jar with a tight fitting lid combine the lemon juice, lemon zest, honey, vinegar, thyme, olive oil, salt, and pepper. Screw on the lid and shake well. Keeps covered in the refrigerator for 1 week. Makes about a cup.

Fresh Raspberries with Crème Fraîche

Brilliant, bittersweet berries are the very essence of spring. Tame them with the richness of crème fraîche or lightly sweetened sour cream.

SERVES 6

2   pints fresh raspberries
1   cup crème fraîche (recipe follows)
2   teaspoons sugar

Gently rinse the berries. Divide among 6 small dessert bowls or sherbet glasses. Stir the sugar into the crème fraîche. Dollop a tablespoon of crème fraîche over each serving and pass the remaining as desired.

Crème Fraîche

1   cup heavy cream
1   tablespoon buttermilk

In a small bowl mix together the cream and buttermilk. Cover and let sit until thickened, usually overnight, possibly as long as 2 days.

15.

Mother's Day Brunch

My mother relates her most vivid memory of Mother's Day as one in which all three of us (her young daughters) tried to outdo one another in daughterly devotion. We jockeyed for attention with hand-made cards, bickered over how to set the table, squabbled over who sat where at church, etc., etc. Daddy eventually lost his patience and yelled at all of us. At the end of the day, Mama escaped and walked alone up the hill to the dead end, where she sat down, put her head in her hands, and sobbed.

We were a few years older when we learned of this, and had already adopted a more moderate approach in our devotion. Now Mother's Day is a nice excuse to get together for brunch. Daddies do the dishes.

The Menu

Champagne Cocktails

Wilted Watercress and Arugula Salad

Smoked Trout Cakes

Scrambled Eggs with Mushrooms

Rhubarb and Ginger Pie

Champagne Cocktails

An exceptionally civilized manner in which to toast our labor. Do yourself a favor and use an adequate sparkling wine.

FOR EACH COCKTAIL:

1   *cube sugar*
    Dash bitters
1   *cube ice*
    Champagne
1   *twist lemon*

Place the sugar cube, bitters, and ice in a fluted glass. Pour over the champagne and garnish with the lemon twist.

Wilted Watercress and Arugula Salad

Both of these greens have so much vibrant flavor, a light dressing is all they need.

SERVES 6

¼	pound watercress
¼	pound arugula
¼	cup olive oil
1	shallot, minced
2	tablespoons champagne vinegar
	Salt and freshly cracked black pepper to taste
3	tablespoons toasted almond slices

Clean and dry the watercress and arugula, and place in a salad bowl. In a skillet heat the oil and cook the shallot for a couple of minutes until soft. Pour the oil and shallot directly over the greens. Add the vinegar, salt, and pepper. Garnish with the almond slices and serve immediately.

Smoked Trout Cakes

Credit to Moriah's Daddy for these. We first made them at The Corner Market in 1995 for a Valentine's meal.

MAKES 6 TROUT CAKES, ABOUT 4 OUNCES EACH

FOR THE TROUT:

4	smoked trout fillets
1/2	cup cream
1	tablespoon thinly sliced chives
1/4	teaspoon cayenne pepper
	Juice of 1 lemon
2	tablespoons butter

FOR THE CAPER SAUCE:

1/2	cup sour cream
1/4	cup mayonnaise
2	tablespoons coarsely ground mustard
1	tablespoon capers, chopped

Remove the trout from the skin, breaking into about 1-inch pieces and removing any bone. Place in a bowl along with the cream, chives, cayenne, and lemon juice. Stir to mix. The trout will naturally break up. Don't over mix, or it will turn into a paste. I like the cakes with at least some lumps, but the mixture must also hold together. You may play with it a bit and test-cook a small amount to get it right.

In a nonstick frying pan melt the butter until bubbly but not browning. Use an ice cream scoop or ladle to spoon about 4-ounce cakes into the butter. Cook about 4 minutes per side, then drain on paper. Serve hot with the caper sauce. You may keep the cakes warm in a low oven for 30 or so minutes.

To prepare the caper sauce, in a medium bowl stir together the sour cream, mayonnaise, mustard, and capers. Refrigerate until ready to serve. Makes 1 cup.

Scrambled Eggs with Mushrooms

Very simple and utterly delicious. The most prolific local wild mushroom is the heavenly morel. Cultivated "wild" mushrooms are readily available, and more flavorful than buttons.

SERVES 6

3	tablespoons butter
½	onion, diced
½	pound fresh mushrooms
2	cloves garlic
9	eggs
½	cup water
	Salt and pepper to taste
1	tablespoon chopped fresh parsley

In a large nonstick frying pan heat the butter and sauté the onion for about 3 minutes. Add the mushrooms and garlic, toss, and cook on high for about 5 minutes until the mushrooms have given off their liquid and dried somewhat. Meanwhile, crack the eggs into a large bowl. Add about ½ cup of water, salt, pepper, and parsley, and beat well. Pour over the mushroom mixture. Use a wooden spoon to continually lift the cooked part of the egg, letting raw egg run onto the surface of the pan. Cook until set and serve immediately.

Rhubarb and Ginger Pie

I love the fresh taste of rhubarb. The ginger is a sparkling addition.

Serves 6 to 8

5	cups chopped rhubarb (2 pounds fresh rhubarb stalks)
1	cup sugar
¼	cup finely chopped crystallized ginger
¼	cup cornstarch
	Grated zest of 2 lemons
	"Cookie" Pie Pastry (recipe follows)
	Cream
	Sugar

Preheat the oven to 425°. In a large bowl combine the rhubarb, sugar, ginger, cornstarch, and lemon zest, stir, and let sit for 15 minutes. Pile into the refrigerated pie shell. Roll out the remaining pastry to a circle ⅛ inch thick. Use a sharp knife to slice this into 1-inch strips. Place these over the pie, forming a lattice. Trim the edges and crimp with a fork. Brush the top of the pastry with the cream and sprinkle with sugar. Place the pie in the oven and immediately reduce the heat to 375°. Bake for about 1 hour until the crust is browned and the pie juices bubbly and thickened.

"Cookie" Pie Pastry

MAKES A DOUBLE 9-INCH PIE PASTRY

3   cups all-purpose flour
¼   cup sugar
¼   teaspoon salt
½   cup (1 stick) cold butter, cut into bits
⅔   cup shortening
⅓   cup boiling water

In a large bowl stir together the flour, sugar, and salt. Make a well in the center and place the butter and shortening in the well. Pour the boiling water into the well and use a fork to stir together the water and fats until most of the fats have melted. Now stir the flour mixture into the liquid and fat with the fork. Gather the dough together on a floured work surface. Divide the dough into 2 pieces. Shape these into discs. Wrap in plastic and chill at least 1 hour, or up to 1 day. Let the dough soften slightly before rolling out.

16.

Graduation Dinner

Graduation marks the end of an era as well as the beginning of a new one. It is a worthy event—a time to celebrate achievements as well as friendships. I remember graduation as bittersweet, as well. While I looked forward to more exciting times, I realized that things would never be the same, even with the friends I managed to keep. I wasn't concerned for the future. The future would take care of itself, but I was frightened of stepping out of my past. Scared to leave friends with whom I'd gone to school for seven years. I was instinctively worried that I hadn't appreciated them all enough, that I would forget the important secrets we had shared.

Graduates deserve congratulations and familial support: faith in their abilities to test the rising waters. Treat them with a special, very grown-up dinner party with a few of their close friends.

The Menu

Grilled Veal Chops with Shiitakes

———

Mint and Orange Relish

———

Asparagus and Leek Gratin

———

Dense Chocolate Almond Cake

Grilled Veal Chops with Shiitakes

Veal chops are wonderful on the grill. Charring the outside develops the mild flavor, while a quick cook keeps the tender meat nice and moist.

I chose shiitake mushrooms because I am privy to some incredibly tasty organic ones that are grown locally on oak logs. Any wild mushroom would do nicely.

SERVES 6

6	veal chops
½	pound shiitake mushrooms
¼	cup plus 1 tablespoon olive oil
3	cloves garlic, pressed or finely minced
2	bay leaves
	Salt and black and white pepper to taste
	Juice of ½ lemon
½	pound mixed baby greens, rinsed and spun dry
	Mint and Orange Relish (recipe follows)

Rinse the veal chops and pat dry. Dust any loose dirt from the shiitakes and remove the tough stems. In a shallow bowl mix together ¼ cup of olive oil, the garlic, bay leaves, salt, and pepper. Add the chops and mushrooms, turning to coat. Refrigerate for 1 to 8 hours.

Meanwhile, prepare a grill to medium heat. Remove the chops from the marinade. Wrap the bones of the chops in aluminum foil so they they don't burn. Cook the chops about 5 minutes per side for medium rare. Salt and pepper the mushrooms and grill for a total of 4 minutes. Toss with the remaining 1 tablespoon of olive oil and the lemon juice. Divide the greens among the plates. Place the mushrooms over the baby greens, laying the chop (aluminum foil removed) to one side. Drizzle the Mint and Orange Relish over all, and pass the remaining relish.

Mint and Orange Relish

Fresh tasting and very pretty. Really a salad in itself. Try it spooned over goat cheese as an appetizer.

SERVES 6

	Zest and flesh of 3 medium oranges
3	*cloves garlic, pushed through a press*
½	*red onion, diced small*
	Juice of ½ lemon
¼	*cup olive oil*
3	*tablespoons chopped fresh mint*
	Salt and black and red pepper to taste
	Dash ground cinnamon

Use a zester to remove the orange zest in thin strips. Use a sharp paring knife to cut away all the white pith. Working over a bowl, section the oranges, pushing each section down and out with a paring knife. Add the remaining ingredients, including the zest. Stir and season to taste. Serve at room temperature. Keeps in the refrigerator, covered, for about 3 days.

Asparagus and Leek Gratin

A rich and savory preparation for asparagus. Sure to be a hit.

SERVES 6

1	tablespoon butter
1	tablespoon all-purpose flour
1	cup milk, heated
	Salt and white pepper to taste
	Pinch grated nutmeg
1	pound asparagus
1	bunch leeks, white part only
3	ounces fresh goat cheese
3	tablespoons fresh bread crumbs

In a saucepan melt the butter. Sprinkle in the flour, whisking. Slowly pour in the heated milk, continuing to whisk. Heat to a boil, turn down to simmer, and cook the sauce for 30 minutes. Season with the salt, pepper, and nutmeg.

Meanwhile, rinse the asparagus and snap the stem off where it begins to toughen. Steam in a covered steamer or colander over salted, simmering water for about 1 minute only. Slice the leeks in half lengthwise. Rinse well under running water, separating each layer. (They can be very sandy.) Slice crosswise in thin half circles. Steam for about 5 minutes until tender.

Preheat the oven to 400°. Butter a shallow casserole. Spread the asparagus over the bottom of the casserole and top with the leeks. Spoon the sauce over the vegetables. Break up the cheese and scatter over the sauce. Top with the bread crumbs. Bake until lightly browned and bubbly, about 15 to 20 minutes.

Dense Chocolate Almond Cake

A chocolate lover's dream!

SERVES ABOUT 10

1   cup almond slices, toasted
1   cup (2 sticks) unsalted butter
8   ounces semi or bittersweet chocolate
8   eggs, separated
1¼   cups sugar
1   tablespoon almond liqueur (or 1 teaspoon almond
     extract)
     Confectioners' sugar

Preheat the oven to 325°. Grease and flour a 10-inch springform pan. In a food processor grind the almonds. In the top of a double boiler over simmering heat melt the butter and chocolate together, stirring frequently. In a bowl whisk the eggs yolks with 1 cup of the sugar until light. Whisk the chocolate mixture into the yolks. Stir in the almonds and liqueur.

Beat the egg whites to soft peak. Sprinkle over the remaining sugar and beat until stiff. Fold a bit of the chocolate into the egg whites, then gently fold the whites into the remaining chocolate. Pour the batter into the prepared pan and bake for about 1 hour. When tested, the center of the cake will still be slightly moist. Let the cake cool and settle into the pan. Remove the rings from the pan. Dust with confectioners' sugar and serve, cut into wedges.

Index

INDEX